Watch It Grow

# A Penguin's Life

### Nancy Dickmann

Heinemann Library
Chicago, Illinois

**www.heinemannraintree.com**
Visit our website to find out more information about Heinemann-Raintree books.

**To order:**
☎ Phone 888-454-2279
🖥 Visit www.heinemannraintree.com to browse our catalog and order online.

Edited by Nancy Dickmann, Rebecca Rissman, and Catherine Veitch
Designed by Joanna Hinton-Malivoire
Picture research by Mica Brancic
Production by Victoria Fitzgerald
Originated by Capstone Global Library
Printed and bound in China by South China Printing Company Ltd

15 14 13 12 11 10
10 9 8 7 6 5 4 3 2 1

**Library of Congress Cataloging-in-Publication Data**
Dickmann, Nancy.
  A penguin's life / Nancy Dickmann. -- 1st ed.
    p. cm. -- (Watch it grow)
  Includes bibliographical references and index.
  ISBN 978-1-4329-4230-4 (hc) -- ISBN 978-1-4329-4233-5 (pb) 1.
Penguins--Life cycles--Juvenile literature. I. Title.
QL696.S47D53 2011
  598.47--dc22
                          2010000091

**Acknowledgments**
We would would like to thank the following for permission to reproduce photographs: Ardea pp. **7** (Graham Robertson), **9** (Auscape); FLPA p. **16** (Minden Pictures/Ingo Arndt); Nature Picture Library pp. **5** (© Fred Olivier), **21** (© David Tipling); Photolibrary pp. **4** (Flirt Collection/Kevin Dodge), **6** (Oxford Scientific Films (OSF)/Kjell Sandved), **8** (Oxford Scientific Films (OSF)/David Tipling), **10** (Cusp/Frank Krahmer [Oxford Scientific Films (OSF)/David Tipling]), **11** (Oxford Scientific Films (OSF)/Mike Tracey), **12** (Picture Press/Thorsten Milse), **13** (age fotostock/Morales Morales), **14** (Oxford Scientific Films (OSF)/Tui De Roy), **15** (Oxford Scientific Films (OSF)/Tui De Roy), **17** (Oxford Scientific Films (OSF)/Doug Allan), **18** (All Canada Photos/Wayne Lynch), **19** (Oxford Scientific Films (OSF)/Doug Allan), **20** (Tsuneo Nakamura), **22 bottom** (Oxford Scientific Films (OSF)/Tui De Roy), **22 left** (Oxford Scientific Films (OSF)/Tui De Roy), **22 right** (Picture Press/Thorsten Milse), **22 top** (Oxford Scientific Films (OSF)/David Tipling), **23 bottom** (Oxford Scientific Films (OSF)/Mike Tracey), **23 middle bottom** (Picture Press/Thorsten Milse), **23 middle top** (age fotostock/Morales Morales), **23 top** (Oxford Scientific Films (OSF)/Tui De Roy).

Front cover photograph of emperor penguins in Antarctica reproduced with permission of Corbis (© Paul Souders). Inset photograph of an emperor penguin egg reproduced with permission of Photolibrary (Oxford Scientific (OSF)/David Tipling). Back cover photograph of an emperor penguin with an egg reproduced with permission of Ardea (Graham Robertson).

The publishers would like to thank Nancy Harris for her assistance in the preparation of this book.

Every effort has been made to contact copyright holders of material reproduced in this book. Any omissions will be rectified in subsequent printings if notice is given to the publishers.

# Contents

# Life cycles

All living things have a life cycle.

Penguins have a life cycle.

A chick hatches. It grows into a penguin.

egg

A penguin lays eggs. Later it will die.

# Eggs

A female penguin lays an egg in winter.

egg

She gives the egg to a male penguin.

It is very cold in winter.

egg under skin

The male penguin keeps the egg
warm on his feet.

# Chicks

A chick hatches from the egg.

Its parent gives it food.

The chick has fluffy gray feathers.
Soon they fall out.

There are white and black feathers under the gray ones.

# Becoming a Penguin

The young penguin learns to swim.

The young penguin catches fish
to eat.

The penguins walk across the ice
in fall.

They meet up in a big group.

A female penguin lays an egg.

The life cycle starts again.

# Life Cycle of a Penguin

1. A female penguin lays an egg.

2. A chick hatches from the egg.

3. The chick grows bigger.

4. The chick becomes an adult.

22

# Picture Glossary

 **feather** body covering on birds

 **female** able to have babies. A girl is a female.

 **hatch** to be born from an egg

 **male** able to be a father. A boy is a male.